RUNNYMEDE

A PICTORIAL HISTORY

Richard Williams

INTRODUCTION

Since the publication of our first picture book in 1988, members of the Egham-by-Runnymede Historical Society have been repeatedly asked 'when are you going to publish something about Runnymede?' Well, the book you are holding has been produced in response to those requests and we sincerely hope it answers many questions as well as filling in the gaps left by other locally produced books. It was never intended to be a definitive history of the famous meadow or, indeed, cover all the public events ever held there. We are obviously restricted by the photographs and illustrations available, but most major events are represented within the eight sections of the book. Despite being known throughout the world as the birthplace of freedom under the law, as far as we are aware, Runnymede has never before been the subject of a single volume.

It is appropriate therefore that the Egham-by-Runnymede Historical Society has published this book. Using a combination of local knowledge and historical fact it is illustrated with a number of previously unpublished pictures, with reproduction in colour where colour exists. In keeping with modern trends I have referred to the whole meadow as Runnymede in the final two sections.

Richard Williams, July 1995.

ACKNOWLEDGEMENTS

The author is most grateful to the following people and institutions for all their help and encouragement during the preparation of this book. In particular, the members of the Egham-by-Runnymede Historical Society including Dorothy & Ron Davis, Graham Dennis, Diana Fear, Cyril Greenslade, John Hardaker, Don Kirby, John Mills (Hon. Curator, Egham Museum), Kathleen Trower, Jill Williams (who also did the typesetting) and Ronald Wykes. Others include Jonathan Bingham (Ian Allan Printing), Peter Booton, WLC Branford, Elsie Cannon, Amanda Devonshire (Curator, Chertsey Museum), Ann den Engelse (The National Trust), The British Library, The Egham Museum Trust, Lord Fairhaven, Jim Godwin, Imperial War Museum, Robin Lewis (The National Trust), Anna Mason (The Kennedy Memorial Trust), Sarah Pickering (Pitkin Pictorials Ltd), Norman Pollard, The Trustees of the S A Oliver Charitable Settlement, Graham Snelling (The National Horse Racing Museum), Nino Strachey (The National Trust), Angela Walton (Staines and Egham News), Tim Williams (Runnymede Borough Council) and many others who have made this book a reality. Photographic credits appear in the text. Where any possibility of copyright ownership exists attempts have been made to contact the owner(s). Apologies are due if any do exist of which the publishers are not aware.

Egham-by-Runnymede Historical Society is a Registered Charity No. 257294. Net proceeds from the sale of this book will be used to further its charitable purposes.

CONTENTS

RUNNYMEDE-Aerial view from Cooper's Hill looking east *c 1950*

In geological terms, Runnymede is just one of many flood plains along the river Thames. For this reason the nearby town of Egham grew up a safe distance away to the south of the river, rather than along its banks as did so many other towns. The name Runnymede is probably derived from the Anglo-Saxon word, *Rune*, meaning municipal or council and *Mead*, a derivation of meadow, an area of grassland cut annually for hay. Runnymede is not mentioned by name in the Domesday survey of 1086 but would have been surveyed as part of the Manor of Egham, held by Chertsey Abbey since AD 666. The first mention of the name Runnymede appears in the Magna Carta document of 1215, suggesting that it was already well established as a place-name at that date.

Nowadays the whole meadow tends to be referred to as Runnymede, but on early maps and surveys the western end towards Windsor is usually called Long Mead, suggesting a clearer line of demarcation in earlier times. Locally produced maps of the 19th century show a portion of land between Runnymede and Long Mead as Ride Mead, but this appears to be of only local significance and may have had something to do with the horse racing held there in the 18th and 19th centuries. This central area is recorded as being used as arable land for over 200 years. This aerial view of Runnymede shows the slopes of Cooper's Hill in the foreground with part of Langham Pond visible at the foot of the hill just below the line of trees.
The Egham Museum Trust

3

MANOR MAP *based on an 1802 survey*

At the time of the Domesday survey, practically the whole of Surrey was technically within Windsor Forest and therefore subject to the Forest Laws. However, the Manor of Egham was held by Chertsey Abbey and William the Conqueror granted the Abbot of Chertsey certain hunting privileges. Following the dissolution of the monastery in 1537 Runnymede became Crown Land. By this time, possibly earlier, a number of narrow strips were designated to local inhabitants on both Runnymede and Long Mead. Their exact purpose is unknown but were presumably for crops of some kind rather than grazing. Runnymede was subject to an Enclosure Act in 1814, which, following the required survey, was awarded in 1817. At that time there were 19 tenants with land on Runnymede. The Act stipulated that Runnymede could be stocked with horses and cattle from Old Lammas Day (August 1st) until November 13th and with sheep from November 14th until February 2nd. Between February 3rd and August 1st it was left for hay. The central area of Runnymede was left unenclosed. The Act clearly stated that any enclosure which interfered with the holding of horse racing there each August must be removed.

The Oliver Collection

HAYMAKING ON RUNNYMEDE

Haymaking is known to have been carried out on Runnymede for centuries, reaching a peak during the coaching days of the 18th and early 19th century. Having a ready supply of locally grown hay was a great asset to the stables of the numerous Egham inns. This watercolour by George A Fripp is dated 1865 and shows haymaking on Long Mead with Magna Carta Island clearly shown on the left.

The National Trust

COOPER'S HILL

The first mention of Cooper's Hill appears in a survey of the area carried out between 1547 and 1550. It is thought that the name derived from the Cowper family who probably held land there in the 16th century. Thomas Cowper, a resident of nearby Thorpe, was recorded as being a persistent offender against the Forest Laws during this period. In 1642 a local poet, John Denham, (1615-1669) wrote a poem called *'Cooper's Hill'* which is regarded as the first example in English of a poem devoted to a topographical subject. Cooper's Hill became increasingly popular with 19th century visitors for the views across Runnymede and 'five neighbouring counties'. The spot known as the Look Out, near to the 285 ft summit, was particularly popular. In 1964 the then Egham Urban District Council gave more than 100 acres of the wooded slopes of Cooper's Hill adjoining Runnymede to the National Trust giving them a total of nearly 300 acres at Runnymede.

Richard Williams

VIEWS FROM COOPER'S HILL

This detailed pencil sketch *(above)* is by George Delamotte, a landscape painter and drawing master, and dates from about 1835. It shows a rural scene with sheep and cattle grazing in the foreground on the slopes of Cooper's Hill. Below them, near the river's edge, is a line of eight or so horses ready to pull passing barges upstream towards Windsor. Set in the river beyond them are a number of conical shaped eel-traps arranged on a small weir. When submerged, eels swimming upstream became caught in the basket-like traps where they remained until the fishermen returned to remove the catch. In the centre of the picture is the recently completed house belonging to George Simon Harcourt on Magna Carta Island. On the opposite bank are the wide open spaces of Wraysbury, with little more than the church of St Andrew's to be seen.
The Egham Museum Trust

A photograph taken in the 1930s *(above right)* looking east across Runnymede towards Staines.
The Egham Museum Trust

A hand-coloured print of about 1850 *(right)* showing the view across Long Mead, with Windsor Castle in the background.
Graham Dennis Collection

MAGNA CARTA ISLAND

Strictly speaking, Magna Carta Island is in the County of Berkshire (formerly Buckinghamshire) and does not form part of Runnymede. However it is included here as it has many links with the Surrey side of the river. During the 16th century the island was occupied by William Danby and his family. They held fisheries between Magna Carta Island and Runnymede and also operated the Ankerwyke ferry, a service maintained by various ferrymen until about 1850. The accommodation on the island in Danby's time would have been no more than a simple fisherman's cottage. The name Magna Carta Island probably only goes back to the 18th century and may have been given by the Harcourt family who lived there until about 1850. This print of about 1860 shows the house built by George Simon Harcourt in 1834. He was Lord of the Manor of Ankerwyke Purnish and held several pieces of land in Surrey, near to Runnymede. It is said that some of the stone for the house came from Marlow Church, a few miles upstream, and included what Harcourt called the Charter Stone. This was octagonal in shape and measured about 3ft in diameter. It was placed permanently in one room and inscribed 'Be it remembered that on this island on 25 June 1215 (sic) John, King of England, signed Magna Carta and in the year 1834 this building was erected in commemoration of that great and important event by George Simon Harcourt Esq., Lord of the Manor, and then High Sheriff of the County'. Nowadays, historians think it unlikely that the meeting between the king and the barons would have taken place on an island.
Graham Dennis Collection

LANGHAM POND

Langham Pond, a narrow stretch of water to the south of the Thames, may at one time have been connected to the river itself. Whether it once formed part of an earlier river-course cannot be said with any certainty. Before the days of locks and river management, the route of the Thames at Runnymede would have been less easily defined, especially when water levels rose in winter months. The present river channel probably has not changed significantly since Saxon times (400-800AD), although it is possible that Runnymede itself often became an island as the seasons floodwaters encroached. It is likely that the name came from the de Langham family who were known to have resided in Egham during the 14th century, although the precise location of their lands could not be traced. The cul-de-sac known as Langham Place, off Egham High Street, is a comparatively recent name for the small community at the western end of the town.
Richard Williams

AN ELEGANT FISHING PARTY NEAR MAGNA CARTA ISLAND FROM RUNNYMEDE

his watercolour by Thomas Rowlandson (1756-1827) can be dated to about 1803, a period when the artist s known to have been working near London on subjects for *'The Microcosm of London'* a work ubsequently published in 1808. While on sketching trips, Rowlandson often visited the Thames, articularly the area near to Runnymede. An earlier work dated 1784 and entitled *'Breakfast at Egham'* is believed to show the interior of the old Catherine Wheel inn. This earlier painting is in the Henry E Huntingdon Library and Art Gallery, San Marino, California, USA.

Thomas Rowlandson was one of a large group of competent draughtsmen of the period. The combination of humour and feeling with which he portrayed the life and customs of the period was uniquely his own, making them important social documents as well as creations of beauty. The watercolour was purchased by The Egham Museum Trust in May 1980 and is on permanent display in The Egham Museum.

The Egham Museum Trust

9

BELL WEIR LOCK *1910*

Before the introduction of a lock system the Thames was tidal as far as Staines Bridge. The site for Bell Weir Lock was chosen in order to make use of a natural gravel bank close to the southern bank, thus providing a narrow channel for the construction of the lock. The accompanying weir was built across the wider stretch of water to the north. The lock system here was built at a cost of £6,650 and was first opened during the winter of 1817-18. The name was derived from Charles Bell, the first lock-keeper, who may have been living in a small cottage close by. By 1843 the lock-keeper, now Henry Fennimore, was recorded as living in 'the lock house' dating the present building to about that time. It is probable that the earlier cottage, was then extended to become the Anglers' Rest, certainly the increasing number of river users would have welcomed a place of refreshment so conveniently close to the lock.

Bell Weir Lock was not without its problems in the 19th century. In 1827 just years after it opened, the weir was badly damaged by ice. Both the weir and the lock were completely rebuilt following extensive flood damage in 1867-8 and again in 1877. Markers on the lock-keepers cottage record the exceptional heights reached by the floods of 1894 and 1947. With the highest ever recorded rainfall for January and February in 1995 the 50 year cycle may have been extended had it not been for greater flood control measures.

More recently, the weir was rebuilt in 1961 and the lock modernised and enlarged between October 1973 and June 1974.

Jill Williams Collection

THE ANGLERS' REST *c 1960*

The Anglers' Rest, seen here from the towpath, would have been a popular place for refreshment both for the many 19th century bargemen regularly using the river and the growing number of weekend visitors who were discovering the pleasures of boating.

Its close proximity to Bell Weir Lock made it a convenient spot to take a well earned break. The name Anglers' Rest suggests it was popular with local fishermen too. It is thought that some type of building stood on this site in the early years of the 19th century which may have become the lock-keeper's cottage when Bell Weir Lock first opened in 1817-18. The name Anglers' Rest appears in 1856 with the freehold being held by a brewer named as Thomas Harris. The building shown in the photograph dates from about this time and may have contained parts of the earlier structure. It was completely demolished in 1973 and the Runnymede Hotel built on the site.

The Egham Museum Trust

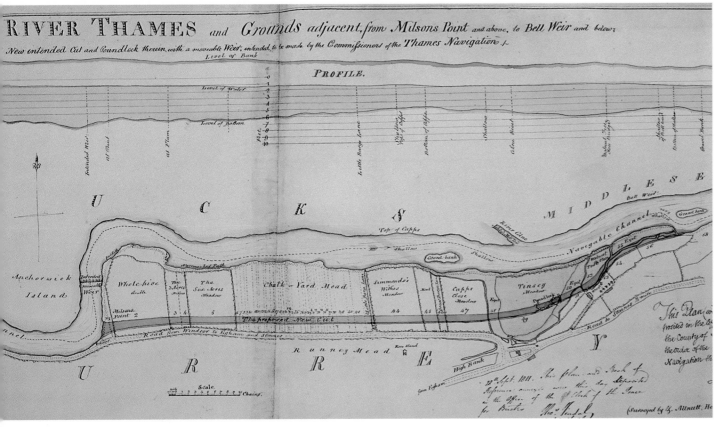

YARD MEAD AND MILSON'S POINT *The proposed cut of 1811*

Maps of the late 18th and early 19th century show a small area between the river Thames and Runnymede divided into small agricultural plots called Yard Mead. In 1811, shortly before the opening of Bell Weir Lock, a cut or channel was proposed in order to assist the flow of the river and therefore help avert serious flooding during the winter months. This channel, had it been cut, would have effectively made Yard Mead and the surrounding area an island, giving limited access to those depending on it for their livelihood. The proposal was later dropped. Yard Mead gradually became developed later in the 19th century and the name disappeared from common use. However, it survives as the name of a cul-de-sac leading from the Windsor Road (A308) to a small marina and boatyard. The gravel bank shown on the map played an important part during the construction of Bell Weir Lock in 1816-18 by creating a natural dividing line between the lock and the weir.
Buckinghamshire County Record Office (Ref. P/u A25)

RUNNYMEDE IN FLOOD *1915*

Before river management became as sophisticated as it is today, the river Thames burst its banks almost annually, often to substantial depths as shown in this photograph of 1915. During such periods, the road to Windsor (A308), no more than a track before the mid 19th century, was impassable. The alternative route took the traveller through Englefield Green. As far as can be remembered, this part of the A308 was last flooded in January 1959. (See back cover). Since then, improved techniques for dredging and in river flow control has ensured that any sudden rise in water levels is more effectively controlled and major flooding avoided.
The Egham Museum Trust

EGHAM BY-PASS   *1947*

Like a number of other small towns, nearby Egham grew by virtue of being on a main trunk road between London and the south and west of England. The town had become popular during the coaching days of the 18th and early 19th century, with a large number of inns catering for visitors as they passed through the town. During the inter-war years of the 20th century motorised vehicles began to dominate the roads and Egham town centre became increasingly congested. This led to the construction of a by-pass on the northern side of the town, completed in 1935. The route chosen for the new road followed the remains of a 13th century man-made embankment that originally stretched from Staines Bridge to the foot of Cooper's Hill in order to protect the town of Egham from flood water. The elevated pathway along the Causeway between Egham and Staines is also part of the original embankment. The only time that floodwater reached the Egham by-pass was in March 1947 as shown in this photograph. Although flooded for about 48 hours the road remained open to traffic. The by-pass was up-graded to a dual carriageway in the 1960s.
Richard Williams Collection

PARIPAN PAINT WORKS *1950s*

Originally, this three acre site on Yard Mead had been made up of three small plots used as pasture. During 1866 a Robert Spice purchased the three plots and built a factory there. By the end of 1867 the property was occupied by the West Surrey Chemical Works and they remained there until the Copal Varnish Company took over the site between 1875-76. Ten years later Randall Brothers, manufacturers of colours for the printing ink and paint industries, purchased the Copal Varnish Company and within two years moved all their production from Bankside near London Bridge to the Yard Mead site. The name Paripan was derived from 'Paris White Japan', an enamel manufactured by the Company, first registered as a trade name in 1900. The conversion from a private family business to a public company under the name Paripan Ltd. took place in 1919. Manufacturing a wide range of household and industrial paints and varnishes, Paripan Ltd. continued trading until 1962 when a merger with Carson Paints of Battersea was agreed and the company became Carson-Paripan Ltd. By 1967 all production at Yard Mead had ceased and the site, in its final years, was used only for storage. It closed in 1971. The entire site was cleared and by 1973 was re-developed as a warehouse for Citroën Motors. More recently it became a warehouse for Inter-City Transport.
The Egham Museum Trust

RUNNYMEDE HOTEL *1974*

Following the demolition of the Anglers' Rest in 1973, the modern 4 star Runnymede Hotel was built on the site, with the first phase opening to the public later that year. One of the bars in the hotel has been named 'Charlie Bell's', after the 19th century lock keeper at nearby Bell Weir Lock. The hotel offers a large restaurant, known as the River Room, as well as a health and fitness spa, which is open to both residents and non-residents.

The British Museum carried out a number of archaeological digs, at a site near to the hotel at Runnymede Bridge, between 1976 and 1990. The earliest finds included the remains of a Middle Neolithic settlement (about 3000BC). A number of 9th and 8th century BC post-holes were found, indicating a degree of permanancy in the area at that time. In addition, the discovery of artefacts from the Bronze and Iron Ages (1900 to 500BC) have given the area a longer history of occupation than had been previously realised. This photograph was taken in November 1974 when much of the grounds were flooded.
Richard Williams

KING IOHN.

KING JOHN   *18th century print*

Magna Carta, or the Great Charter of English liberty, is synonymous with Runnymede as being the venue for the historic meeting between King John and the 25 barons, in June 1215. The barons were landowners and, as such, were becoming increasingly impatient with the king over the amount of money he was collecting from them in order to fight a series of unsuccessful wars abroad. This money was collected by exerting higher taxation on them and, the way the law stood, they had no alternative but to pay. Collections were both arbitary and extortionate with reprisals against defaulters often ruthless and brutal. It was customary for medieval kings to make their most solemn and binding laws by way of a charter to their subjects and it was by this method the barons thought they had the best chance of changing their destiny. With no reliable contemporary reports available, it is impossible for us to know the exact details of the events that took place on Runnymede. We know that the barons had an encampment at Staines while King John and his retinue were staying at Windsor Castle.The two sides met somewhere on Runnymede during the days leading up to 15 June 1215 but the precise spot is not known. The barons drew up a list of agreements with the king in a document known as the Articles of the Barons. It was to the final version of this document that King John was to attach his seal at Runnymede on 15 June. Copies of the Articles of the Barons were then passed to the legal draughtsmen who amplified them into the form of a charter. The meeting on Runnymede broke up on 23 June and on 24 June, or soon after, seven copies of Magna Carta (exemplifications) were issued from Runnymede with a further six copies being issued from Oxford on 22 July.

It seems that almost immediately, King John dispatched envoys to Pope Innocent III claiming that the Great Charter had been compelled upon him by force and fear. By the end of September 1215 the king's envoys returned from Rome bringing with them solemn bulls (a papal edict) dated 24 and 25 August in which the Pope declared the whole contract to be null and void. King John died in October 1216 and a revised form of Magna Carta was issued following the coronation of his nine year old son as Henry III. Eight years later, in 1225, Magna Carta was re-issued for a third time, but still without full agreement. Finally, in the form of Edward I's confirmation of 12 October 1297, a copy of Magna Carta was placed on the statute roll.

Graham Dennis Collection

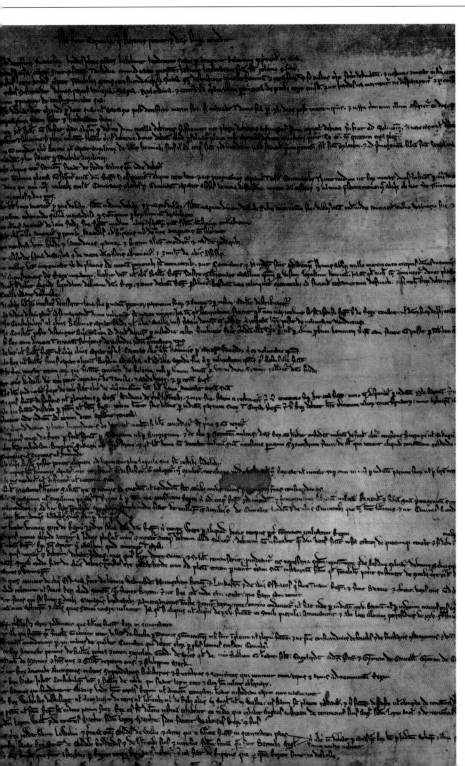

STEPHEN LANGTON *Archbishop of Canterbury*

As Archbishop of Canterbury, Stephen Langton played an important part in the events that led to King John meeting the barons on Runnymede in 1215. His place of birth, about 1155, is unknown. However, there is a public house at Friday Street, a tiny hamlet near Abinger in Surrey, called 'Stephan Langton' lending support to the 19th century legend that this was his birthplace.

When Hubert Walter, Archbishop of Canterbury, died in 1200 the appointment of a successor brought conflict between the monks of Christ Church, Canterbury, the bishops, and the king. Such conflicts were not uncommon but in general the king's will prevailed. The monks chose their sub-prior, Reginald, but the king preferred John de Grey, Bishop of Norwich, a close friend and advisor. Pope Innocent III became involved and at length suggested Stephen Langton to the monks of Christ Church as an Englishman of great learning. John did not agree, but despite this the Pope consecrated the new archbishop near Rome in July 1207. The king refused to confirm the appointment and so Stephen Langton remained on the continent for the next six years. In response to John's attitude the Pope placed England under an interdict. This meant that all church services in the kingdom were suspended, with the exception of baptisms of infants and confessions of the dying. Later, in 1209, the Pope excommunicated John, which proved to be a much more effective weapon. Eventually, in 1213, King John gave in and Stephen Langton returned to England. He soon became highly respected in both the Church and politics, even apparently by the king. Soon after John's absolution later that year, Stephen Langton was present as the king's representative at the Council of St. Albans, when he read aloud the Charter of Henry I. Following the meeting, the recalcitrant barons declared they would fight for the liberties it contained. Stephen Langton, trusted by the barons, persuaded King John to adopt a peaceful and legal means in dealing with them. He later acted as mediator in settling the terms of Magna Carta with the king, turning a purely self-centred baronial document into the Great Charter. Following the bulls of August in which the Charter was annulled, Stephen Langton was suspended by the Pope for failing to secure Magna Carta as a lasting document. Stephen Langton died in 1228 in his early 70s. His arms, shown here, are incorrect. The practice of impaling the archbishop's own arms with those of the See of Canterbury began over 100 years later in 1349.

The Egham Museum Trust

STEPHAN LANGTON

THE INN SIGN AT FRIDAY STREET.

Richard Williams

THE ARTICLES OF THE BARONS

Reproduced by kind permission of the British Library (Additional MS 4838)

William de Hardell

William de Hardell was the mayor of London during the year in which Magna Carta was sealed. At that time the sympathy of Londoners was with the barons and it was for that reason that de Hardell was appointed to ensure its success, with particular reference to the interests of the citizens of London. He was never elevated to the peerage proper, as far as can be ascertained.

William Mallet, Baron of Curry Mallet and Shepton Mallet in Somerset

An ancestor of William Mallet, also called William, was a companion of William the Conqueror and was actually charged by him with the burial of King Harold after the Battle of Hastings. The contemporary chronicler, William of Poitiers, wrote 'the Duke entrusted his body to William Mallet and not to his mother, who offered for her beloved son his weight in gold'.

Richard de Montfitchet

His father had been made Forester of Essex by Henry II but died in 1202 when Richard was only ten years old. In consequence, the boy was made a ward of Richard de Lacy. Richard de Montfitchet was due to inherit the Forests of Essex in June 1215 but had previously joined the rebel barons at Stamford in March of that year causing his estates to be confiscated by the king. Richard recovered his lands, including Ankerwyke near Runnymede where he lived, in October 1217 on returning his allegiance to the Crown. Richard died in 1268 leaving no male heir and his estates passed to his daughter, Aveline, who inherited Wraysbury and Langley. Richard de Montfitchet was the last survivor of the 25 barons.

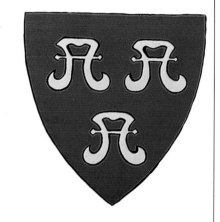

Robert de Ros, Baron de Ros

Robert de Ros, surnamed Farfan, found favour with King John and, with the Bishop of Durham, was deputed to escort William, King of Scotland, into England. Later he became a monk but did not remain a recluse for long as he became the sheriff of Cumberland the following year. When the barons' struggle began he took the side of the king but later changed sides. During the reign of Henry III he seems to have returned his allegiance to the Crown and some of his manors were restored. He married Isabel, the daughter of William the Lion, King of Scotland, and the widow of Robert the Bruce. He died in 1227.

John FitzRobert

John FitzRobert, also known as Baron Warkworth, served as sheriff three times for each of the counties of Northumberland, Norfolk and Suffolk, in the reign of King John. He first sided with the barons and was appointed one of the 25, but afterwards declared his allegiance to the king. He died in 1240.

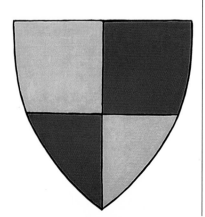

Geoffrey de Say (or Saye), Baron Say

The family originally came from Sai in France, two miles south-east of Argentan in Normandy. William de Say was another noble who came to England with William the Conqueror and yet another William married Beatrix, daughter of Geoffrey de Mandeville. It will be noticed that the de Say coat of arms is the same as that of Geoffrey de Mandeville. Geoffrey de Say, a direct descendent of William, had all his lands in East Anglia and the Midlands seized by the king because of his association with the rebel barons but they were later restored. He died in 1230.

THE MAGNA CARTA

Only four copies of Magna Carta out of the 13 known to have been issued, have survived. Two are in The British Library and one each in Salisbury and Lincoln Cathedral archives. The illustration above is from a copy in The British Library, given to Sir Robert Cotton by Humphrey Wyems (or Wymes) of the Inner Temple on 1 January 1629, and is therefore known as the Cotton Exemplification. According to one account it had been found in a London tailor's shop.

Reproduced by kind permission of The British Library (Cotton Augustus II 106)

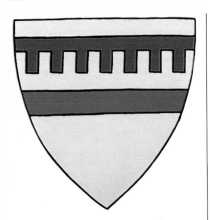

Saher de Quincy

Saher de Quincy was created Earl of Winchester by King John in 1210. He subsequently joined the barons and had principal command at the Battle of Lincoln in May 1217, where he was defeated and taken prisoner. He submitted to Henry III and in the following October all his lands were restored to him. He then proceeded to the Holy Land with the Earls of Chester and Arundel taking part in the Siege of Damietta but dying in 1219 on his way to Jerusalem.

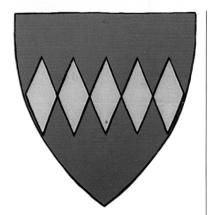

Richard de Percy

This illustrious family were descended from William de Percy, another noble who came to England in 1066. The name is taken from the village of Percy-en-Auge in Normandy. Richard assumed the title on the death of his mother, Agnes, and was the Magna Carta baron, although he did not officially succeed to the title until 1234; hence the use of the ancient arms. He died in 1244.

Eustace de Vesci (or Vescy), Baron de Vesci

Eustace de Vesci succeeded to the title at the age of fourteen following the death of his father, William, in 1184. He was summoned to London by King John in 1213, together with all the other lords suspected of discontent. The king had intended to force them to hand over hostages as a guarantee for their peaceable behaviour but de Vesci, the most aggrieved of the lords, refused and fled to Scotland. His lands were seized and his castle at Alnwick ordered to be demolished. However, in a temporary reconciliation prior to the barons' revolt, de Vesci had his estates restored to him. In 1216 he was hit by an arrow from a crossbow while besieging Barnard Castle and died from his injuries.

William de Lanvellei (or Lanvallei)

Early in the 13th century, William de Lanvellei was in dispute with Hugh de Beauchamp over the ownership of Eaton Socon in Bedfordshire. William's father was Lord of Hallingbury and Stanway in Essex and had been governor of Colchester Castle, which he appeared to have lost in the late 12th century. It was restored to William de Lanvellei shortly after the sealing of Magna Carta when he also obtained the manor of Kingston in Somerset. He died in 1217 without issue.

Richard de Clare, Lord of Clare and 4th Earl of Hertford

The ancestry of this family can be traced back to Geoffrey, a natural son of Richard, Duke of Normandy. The grandson of Geoffrey, Richard FitzGilbert, was given extensive possessions in Suffolk by William the Conqueror as a reward for his participation in the Conquest. FitzGilbert later built a castle at Bury St. Edmunds and his descendents thereafter assumed the title of Earls of Clare.

Gilbert de Clare, Lord of Clare and 5th Earl of Hertford

Gilbert was the son of Richard de Clare and the family shares with the Bigod family the distinction of having two Magna Carta barons. Gilbert later became Earl of Gloucester in the right of his mother, Amicia. He continued his opposition to the arbitary proceedings of the Crown, under Henry III. He fought against the king at Lincoln in 1217 when he was taken prisoner by William Marshall the elder. Soon afterwards he made peace with the king and presumably with William Marshall since he married his daughter Isobel. Gilbert died in 1229.

William Marshall the younger, later Earl of Pembroke

The earliest record of the family is found in the reign of Henry I when Gilbert Mareschall held the office of Marshall to the king, hence taking his surname from the office. William Marshall the elder married Isobel de Clare, only child and heiress of Richard de Clare, the father and grandfather of the Magna Carta barons. The earldom of Pembroke passed to William Marshall with the marriage. He was a supporter of King John but his son, William the younger, supported the baron's cause and became one of the 25. Following the death of King John, William Marshall made peace with Henry III and subsequently fought against the Welsh, heavily defeating Prince Llewellyn. He died in 1231.

John de Lacy (or Lasci), Earl of Lincoln

Another family who came to England with William the Conqueror, they were given Pontefract Castle and other properties in Yorkshire, Nottinghamshire and Lincolnshire. John de Lacy joined forces with the barons but soon made his peace with the king and joined other nobles in the Holy Land. He married Margaret, daughter and co-heiress of Robert de Quincy, Earl of Winchester, and through her was confirmed Earl of Lincoln in 1232. He died in 1240.

Robert de Vere, Earl of Oxford

The first mention of the de Vere family is in the Domesday survey of 1086, where they are shown to have many possessions including Hedingham in Essex, their chief seat, and Chenisiton, now Kensington. Robert, the 3rd Earl, succeeded to the title in 1214 and supported the baron's cause. His wife, Isobel, was the daughter of Walter de Bolebec of Wyrardisbury (Wraysbury). He made his peace with the new king, Henry III, and was appointed a judge in the Court of King's Bench. He died in 1221.

Robert FitzWalter, Lord of Dunmow

Robert FitzWalter was appointed general of the barons' army with the title of Marshall of the Army of God and Holy Church. However, his record was not good and his leadership did not inspire confidence. In 1212 he and Eustace de Vesci had been accused of treasonable activities, were outlawed and their lands seized. FitzWalter's great fortress, Baynard's Castle, near to where St. Paul's Cathedral now stands, was demolished. His opposition to the Crown continued into the reign of Henry III but he was finally defeated at the Battle of Lincoln and taken prisoner. He was, however, soon to be freed as the following year saw him in the Holy Land taking part in the Fifth Crusade and assisting in the siege of Damietta. He died in 1234.

Roger Bigod, Earl of Norfolk

The Bigod family owned land in Essex and Suffolk, including Framlingham in the 11th century. Roger Bigod was a staunch supporter of Richard I and was made one of the ambassadors to Philip of France for obtaining aid towards recovery of the Holy Land. Upon the return of Richard Coeur de Lion from captivity, Roger Bigod, as Earl of Norfolk, assisted at the great council held by King Richard at Nottingham. He served Richard I until that monarch's death in 1199 but sided with the barons against King John. Roger Bigod died in 1220.

Hugh Bigod, later Earl of Norfolk

Hugh was the son of Roger Bigod, denoted by the blue label attached to his coat of arms. The Bigod and the de Clare families share the distinction of having two representatives among the 25 barons. Hugh became the 3rd Earl of Norfolk and married Maud, eldest daughter of William Marshall the elder, father of William Marshall the Magna Carta baron. Hugh died in 1225.

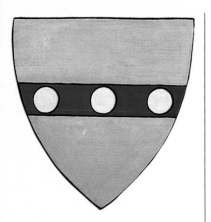

William de Huntingfield, Baron Huntingfield

In the reign of Henry I, Huntingfield manor, near Halesworth in Suffolk, was held by Roger FitzAubrey who assumed the title de Huntingfield. For nearly 250 years the property passed through ten generations in direct succession from father to son alternating between Roger and William until 1377.

Henry de Bohun, Earl of Hertford

Henry de Bohun (pronounced Boon) inherited the office of Constable of England from his father. His lands at Trowbridge in Wiltshire were seized temporarily by King John in 1213 for taking part in the barons' revolt, but were later restored at the sealing of Magna Carta. He was, however, excommunicated by the Pope and was later taken prisoner at the Battle of Lincoln. He married Maud, daughter of Geoffrey FitzPiers, Earl of Essex, and through her, as heiress of her brother William de Mandeville, became Earl of Essex. He died in 1220.

Geoffrey de Mandeville (or Magnavil), Earl of Essex and Gloucester

An earlier Geoffrey de Magnavil arrived in England with William the Conqueror and at the time of the Domesday survey of 1086 owned the whole of Northolt, Perivale, Edmonton, Enfield, Hadley and Ickenham. Geoffrey, the Magna Carta baron, was the eldest son of Geoffrey FitzPiers, descending through his mother and grandmother from the original de Magnavil. He had the title of Earl of Essex conferred upon him by King John and was also granted permission to marry the king's former wife, Isobel, Countess of Gloucester. Thus Geoffrey became Earl of Gloucester through the right of his wife. He died in 1216 following a lance wound, received while attending a tournament in London. The de Mandeville arms are the same as those used by the de Say family.

William d'Aubigney (de Albini), Earl of Arundel

Another family who came from France with William the Conqueror, they held land in Norfolk and elsewhere, including the site where they were to build Castle Rising. William d'Aubigney, the 3rd Earl, was sheriff of the counties of Warwick and Leicester and later Rutland. He was married to Maud, widow of Roger de Clare.

William de Mowbray, Baron Mowbray

The family of Mowbray was founded by the maternal side of the de Albini family by Nigel de Albini in the 11th century. de Albini was granted the lands of Roger de Mowbray who was imprisoned for rebelling against William Rufus and, with the permission of the Pope, married Robert's wife. When the barons' war broke out, William de Mowbray was one of the most prominent lords and was appointed one of the 25. He subsequently fought against the king and was taken prisoner at the Battle of Lincoln.

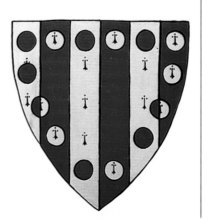

Roger de Montbegan

Roger de Montbegan's ancestors had held land in Lincolnshire during the reign of King Stephen. Roger failed to obtain the lawful right to his lands of Wheatley and Clayworth in Nottinghamshire following Magna Carta and refused to accept the judgement of the court. He angrily withdrew and later ignored a summons issued by the court delivered by knights sent to recall him. His reputation as a baron of the king probably saved him from arrest. He died in 1226 and was suceeded by his cousin, Henry de Montbegon.

The coats of arms are reproduced by permission of The Egham Museum Trust

The author wishes to thank Don Kirby for supplying detailed information on the Magna Carta barons.

MAGNA CARTA *A 19th century print*

A number of 19th century illustrations like this were published showing a
Victorian view of the events on Runnymede in June 1215. Modern historians
doubt whether this much ceremony actually took place.
The Egham Museum Trust

KISS OF PEACE *14th century*

An illustration from a 14th century French manuscript showing King John of England and Philip Augustus, the
French king, exchanging a kiss of peace. This was the medieval equivalent of a handshake, a symbol of trust and
goodwill, and may have formed part of the final ceremonies between King John and the barons at Runnymede.
From a copy in The Egham Museum

William de Forz (or Fortibus), Earl of Albemarle

The 1st Earl of Albemarle was Odo Champagne, who was given the city of Albemarle by the archbishop of Rouen. The male line failed with William, the 3rd Earl, but his daughter, Hawyse, had married William de Mandeville and the earldom passed to him in right of his wife. He died without issue in 1190, and his widow married William de Forz who became the Earl of Albemarle. In October 1214 the king restored the Earl's lands at Skipton and Holderness in Yorkshire and at Cockermouth in Cumberland. Following Magna Carta, his right in the manor of Driffield, Yorkshire, once held by his grandfather, was also restored to him.

THE SEALING OF MAGNA CARTA

King John is the centre figure of this bronze group, attributed to a member of the de Vaulx family and dating from 1870-90. The Archbishop of Canterbury, Stephen Langton, is shown on the left with William de Forz (Fortibus), Earl of Albemarle, on the right.
Chertsey Museum/The Oliver Collection, photograph by John Hardaker

EGHAM RACES ON RUNNYMEDE *1734 - 1884*

Horse racing in England grew rapidly in popularity in the 18th century. Meetings at nearby Ascot had begun in 1711 when formally opened by Queen Anne, and have continued there ever since. With Runnymede so conveniently situated nearby, it was just a matter of time before it too became a venue for horse racing. Referred to as Egham Races, the first recorded event on Runnymede took place over two days in September 1734 and was probably arranged as a local affair by the three contestants. In those early days the contests were referred to as matches rather than races and run over three heats to determine the winner. A second meeting took place in 1735, again over two days, but there is no record of a meeting in 1736; perhaps the ground was unsuitable. It was reinstated in 1737, this time however as a three day event and continued in that format until 1739. An Act of Parliament to prevent the excessive increase in horse racing was passed in 1740 and, together with many other race venues, meetings at Runnymede were suspended. There were two main reasons given for the introduction of the Act. Firstly it was considered detrimental to the sport that so many inferior horses were becoming involved with quality being sacrificed for quantity. Secondly, there was growing concern about the number of men who were being tempted away from their dutiful employment to attend such meetings and, probably worse, encouraged to gamble. The Jockey Club was formed in 1751 as the sport's governing body which led to the introduction of thoroughbred horses in the 1760s. Thus the sport became more respectable and in due course returned to Runnymede under stricter codes of conduct in 1770.

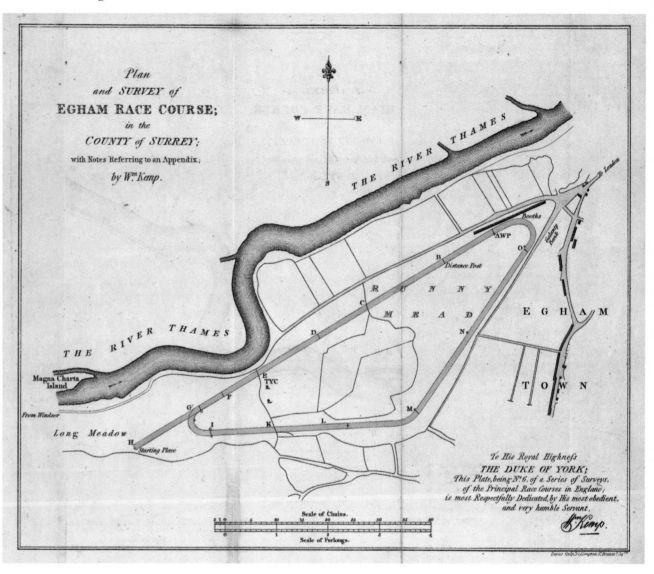

Egham.

On the 24th of *September*, at this Place, a Purse of 20 Guineas was run for, *wt.* 11 *st.* and won by

	H. 1	H. 2
Lord *Portmore's* Grey G.	1	1
Hon. Mr. *Villers's* Grey G. *Sharper*	3	2
Mr. *Archer's* Grey H. *Dangerfield*	2	3

The 10 Guineas, on the following Day, *wt.* 10 *st.* were won by

	H. 1	H. 2
Mr. *Child's* Grey G. *Single-Peeper*	1	1
Mr. *Vincent's* Brown H. *Merry P---le*	2	2
Mr. *Fugger's* Brown H. *Gimlet-Eye*	dis	
Mr. *Wilkins's* Bay H. *Fox*	dis	

Detail of the 1734 entry in the Racing Calendar.

EGHAM RACECOURCE *c 1825*

About 1825, William Kemp produced a plan and survey of the Egham Racecourse at Runnymede, as number six in a series of drawings of the principal racecourses of England. The work was dedicated to His Royal Highness, the Duke of York, reflecting the importance Egham meetings had in racing circles of the time.
Graham Dennis Collection

23

THE LADY AT EGHAM RACES

By the time the sport returned to Runnymede in 1770, the Jockey Club had restructured race meetings by introducing races held over shorter distances. This meant that younger, two and three year old, horses were now being entered, often by wealthy members of the Jockey Club, who were attracted to Runnymede with its close proximity to the established racecourses at Ascot and Windsor. Owners welcomed meetings being held close to one another as horses had to be ridden or walked from one course to the next. A long journey was not the best preparation for an important race. The races themselves were still very primitive; spectators were allowed to wander all over the course in order to obtain the best view of the race. One report referring to a particularly large crowd stated that the contestants weaved their way over the course 'like a dog at a fair'. It was not unusual to see spectators 'keeping up' with the race on horseback. This illustration of *'The Lady at Egham Races'* from a drawing by Richard Barrett Davis (1782 - 1854) was published in 1812 and shows a number of spectators following the race, with the jockeys and their mounts about to pass the winning post. *Graham Dennis Collection*

1822 NOTICE

The popularity of the Egham race meetings on Runnymede reached a peak in the early years of the 19th century. By now, there are references to the annual construction of booths especially for the event and Runnymede as a race venue was beginning to attract its fair share of royal patronage. In 1817 Her Majesty Queen Charlotte, with the princesses, Augusta and Elizabeth, graced the course on the opening day. The meetings also gained additional publicity with the emergence in 1812 of the *Windsor and Eton Express and* *General Advertiser*. Race Balls were held annually either in Windsor or Staines and attracted many famous names from the racing fraternity. By the 1820s, horse racing in England was beginning to resemble the sport we know today, with named races being run by fields of up to a dozen horses. Spectator course invasions were, by now, a thing of the past as stricter safety measures at race meetings were being observed. The illustration, although perhaps containing some artistic licence, gives a good indication of the popularity enjoyed by Egham Races during this period.
Chertsey Museum/The Oliver Collection

EGHAM RACES, 1832.

Second Day, August 29th.

SURREY & MIDDLESEX STAKES

Of TWENTY-FIVE SOVEREIGNS each, 15 ft. and only 5 if declared, &c. Three to remain in, or no race. Two miles and a distance.

Mr I. Day's *Liston*, aged, 9st 3lb *crimson velvet* ....
Sir J. Gibbons na. *Margaret*, 3 yrs. old, 7st. 9lb. *straw color, black cap* ....
Capt. Martyn's *Mistletoe*, 4 yrs. old, 8st. 4lb *purple and orange*
Colonel Challoner na. *Tarquin*, 3 yrs. old, 6st. 10lb. *color unknown*
Mr. Kent's f by *Sultan*, out of *Antiope*, 3 yrs. old, 6st. 7lb. *blue, green cap* ....
Mr. Houldsworth's *Crescent*, 5 yrs. old, 9st. 3lb. ....
Lord Mountcharles' *Arlington*, late *Pilgrim*, 5 yrs. old. 8st. 7lb. .
Capt. Byng's *Ciudad Rodrigo*, 4 yrs. old, 8st. 6lb. ....
Mr. Denison na *Blythe*, 3 yrs old, 7st. 7lb. ....
Lord A. Fitzclarence na. *Hyder*, 3 yrs. old, 6st. 10lb. ....

The following have declared forfeit.

Capt. Ricardo na. *Midhurst*, 4 yrs. old, 8st 7lb.
Duke of Richmond's *Conciliation*, 4 yrs old, 8st. 5lb.
Mr. Cosby's *Hindoo*, 6 yrs old, 8st. 12lb.
Lord Chesterfield's *Marcus*, 4 yrs. old, 8st. 7lb.
Mr. M Ongley's *Pandora*, 5 yrs. old 8st. 4lb.
Mr. Stonehewer na. c. by *Phantom*, dam by *Waterloo*, out of *Ralphina*, 4 yrs old, 8st.
Colonel Salwey na *Zarina*, 4 yrs. old, 7st 13lb.
Mr Gibbons na. b. f. *Lucy*, by *Cain*, 3 yrs. old, 7st. 7lb.
Mr. Scaith na. *Revealer*, by *Reveller*, 3 yrs. old 7st. 7lb.
Mr. Gardnor's bl. f. *Ida*, 4 yrs. old, 8st.

THE MAGNA CHARTA STAKES

Of FIFTY SOVEREIGNS each, h. ft. three yrs. old colts, 8st. 7lb. and fillies, 8st. 4lb. the winner of the Derby, Oaks, or 2000gs. stakes, to carry 7lb. extra. The New Mile.

Sir G. Heathcote's b. c. *Damascus*, by *Reveller*, out of *Jane Shore*, crimson, French grey cap ....
Lord Exeter's b. c. by *Partisan*, out of *Fawn*, light blue ....
Mr. Day's br. f. *L'Amitié*, by *Muley* ....

1832 RACE CARD

The brightly coloured race card for the second day of the 1832 meeting is in complete contrast to the appalling weather experienced that year. It was reported that 'the rain was incessant, the course became ankle deep in mud, the company thin and the sport execrable'. There were reports of attempts being made 'to gammon* gentlemen out of galoshes at inflated prices'. The demand for cloaks, umbrellas and clogs was extensive. Despite the weather, a big attraction in 1832 was Tippoo Sultan's flamboyant and splendid tent, brought from the Woolwich military establishment and erected on Runnymede for the accommodation of the royal party. It had been captured from the Ruler of Mysore after the siege of Seringapatam in 1799.

* to gammon - to hoax or deceive
Chertsey Museum/The Oliver Collection

At a Public Meeting of the Inhabitants of the Parish and Royal Manor of Egham, held at the Assembly Rooms, on Monday, the fifteenth day of August, 1836, COLONEL SALWEY in the Chair:

It was proposed by G. S. Harcourt, Esq. seconded by Colonel Challoner, and unanimously resolved that the following Address be presented to His Majesty.

To the King's most excellent Majesty.

May it please your Majesty,

We, the Inhabitants of the Parish and Royal Manor of Egham, humbly beg permission to approach Your Majesty with sentiments of the most sincere attachment to your Royal Person, and most warmly to express our deep and grateful sense of Your Majesty's gracious condescension and kindness, evinced by the late munificent grant of a Free Plate to our long established Races, by which we not only entertain a confident assurance that their prosperity will be encreased, but that the interests of the Town and Neighbourhood will be essentially promoted.

Under the influence of this feeling, we desire to offer our humble yet heartfelt thanks for the gracious patronage which Your Majesty has been pleased to bestow on us and this our National sport; and for that considerate kindness of heart which (so truly characteristic of your late illustrious Father,) is ever promoting the happiness and welfare of all classes of Your Majesty's subjects.

That Your Majesty and your illustrious Consort may be spared to reign over us in health and happiness for many years, is the earnest and fervent prayer of Your Majesty's dutiful and loyal subjects.

Signed, on behalf of the Meeting,

HENRY SALWEY.

THE LOYAL ADDRESS

In 1836, William IV instituted a one hundred guinea prize, called His Majesty's Plate, which was to be run annually over two miles. In response to this generous gesture, the people of Egham decided to present His Majesty with a Loyal Address in appreciation. It was presented in the Royal Stand by the chairman of the Egham Races Committee, Lieutenant-Colonel Henry Salway, on the first day of the 1836 meeting.
The Egham Museum Trust

WILLIAM IV ARRIVING AT EGHAM RACES

During the reign of George IV (1820-30) Egham Races suffered a number of fluctuations and setbacks. There were many suggestions that it might be better if future meetings were transferred either to Ascot or Windsor. However, the Runnymede venue survived and, following the accession of William IV to the throne in 1830 Egham Races once again enjoyed a period of stability. The king and Queen Adelaide regularly attended race meetings during their short reign. In 1835, the king, having enjoyed his visits there, renewed the lease on the land and permitted all of the area constituting Long Mead and Runnymede to be thrown open. Sadly, 1836 was to be his last visit to Egham Races. King William IV died in June 1837, aged 71, but he had apparently ensured the future of Egham Races for all time. The painting, undated, is by S W Spoade and shows King William IV arriving at the one mile winning post on Long Mead.

Chertsey Museum/The Oliver Collection

EGHAM RACES by HENRY JUTSUM *c 1860*

Following the death of King William IV it was hoped that the young Queen Victoria would continue the royal patronage, but there is no evidence that she ever attended the meetings at Runnymede. Egham Races entered a new period of prosperity following the opening of the Windsor, Staines and South Western Railway in 1848. The special trains from Waterloo were packed with racing enthusiasts and the future of the meeting seemed assured. Egham's own station opened in 1856 but by now the number of pickpockets and confidence tricksters arriving from London were becoming too much for the local police force to control. However, at this time Egham was considered to be the best country race course in England with access by rail from all parts of the country and being held in such pleasant surroundings. Not every one shared the view. John Monsell, vicar of Egham 1853-70, delivered a tirade from his pulpit in 1858 against 'the evils of sports of the turf'. That same year, Charles Dickens published his Christmas Stories and in a passage in *Going into Society* he wrote 'most unexpectedly, the mystery came out one day at Egham Races'. This was the only reference to the races in an otherwise unconnected story. The oil painting by Henry Jutsum (1816-69) of Egham Races c1860, captures the atmosphere of a country race meeting. The view is looking east towards Staines. *Chertsey Museum/The Oliver Collection*

JOCKEY J. JARVIS on ANCHORITE   *1878*

Anchorite, a five year old owned by Mr Quartly, was entered in the Denham Selling Handicap Plate, a five furlong race, at Runnymede in 1878. Here, jockey J Jarvis is shown on Anchorite just prior to the race which was won by Capt. A Paget's Cincinnatus by a head. Anchorite, carrying 7st 11lb (49.5Kg) finished 6th in a field of ten. This is one of many oil paintings by an artist known simply as 'Alan' showing a variety of racing scenes at Runnymede.

Chertsey Museum/The Oliver Collection

EGHAM RACES *c 1880*

During the 1880s crowd control at Egham Races had become almost impossible. In 1881, gangs of up to 25-30 openly insulted and indiscriminately assaulted a large number of spectators, leaving the limited police presence unable to cope. Because the land at Runnymede belonged to the Crown, neither the Jockey Club nor the Egham Races Committee were able to charge spectators admission and therefore had little or no control over those who attended the meetings. So although Runnymede remained a popular venue with owners, jockeys and the public, the rowdy element ensured that the 1884 meeting was the last.

Many of Egham's races were transferred to the newly opened Kempton Park, some fifteen miles away. There is now little evidence that horse racing took place on Runnymede, maybe a few of the metal fences enclosing Ride Mead date from the 19th century, but that is all. A Mr H Gale, talking in 1932, stated that the winning post was only cut down 'three or four years ago' during the tenancy of G J Caddey as it was in the way of hay cutting. This oil painting by 'Alan' captures the scene at Runnymede during the final years at Egham Races.
From a private collection, reproduced with permission

RUNNYMEDE FOR SALE

Why is Runnymede, with its famous historical associations, included in the 7,574 acres which the British Government are offering for sale? The Daily Express gave prominence to the subject on Thursday and it has aroused great public interest. The advertisement states:-

'On the Manor Farm is Runnymede. The armies of King John and the confederate barons encamped here on the signing of the Magna Carta on June 15 1215.' The Government, in offering the ninety nine acres of Runnymede for sale, make capital of the fact that this portion of the estate which forms 'Lot 8' is historic ground.

The natural public outcry that has been raised has resulted in an endeavour by the officials to minimize the historic interests of 'Lot 8'.

"There has been a good deal of misapprehension in regard to Runnymede" said an official of the Commissioners of Woods and Forests to a Daily Express representative yesterday. "The land offered for sale is not Runnymede Island in the Thames where Magna Carta was signed. This island does not belong to the Crown and as far as is known, never has. Runnymede, which comprises Lot 8 in this sale is ninety nine acres of meadow land on the south side of the Thames and is half a mile away from the famous Island."

The official referred to the Ordnance Survey which states that Magna Carta was signed on the island and not on the meadow on the south bank of the river.

The public want to know two things:-
Why are these lands to be sold?
What is to be done with the money that they realise?
A Government official to whom these questions were put yesterday replied "They are being sold in the interests of the taxpayer. More than that I cannot say".

From The Daily Express, Saturday 6 August 1921

MRS HELENA NORMANTON (1882 - 1957)
Secretary of the Magna Carta Society (1921 - 1951)

As a means of raising money to offset the expense of the First World War, the government of the day planned to sell 7,574 acres of land, nationwide. Of this, 252 acres were Crown Land, and included 99 acres at Runnymede. It was those 99 acres, known as 'Lot 8', which attracted the attention of Mrs Helena Normanton, a member of the Middle Temple, while perusing the Parliamentary Papers of forthcoming events. Mrs Normanton immediately brought the proposed sale to the attention of the Press Association and on 4 August 1921 'Runnymede for sale' made front page news. She also wrote to A C Tranter, vicar of Egham, and visited the Marquess of Lincolnshire, KG, a landowner near to Runnymede, in order to gain support against the sale. Their efforts quickly gathered momentum. Support was not just from local residents fearful that the area might be turned into a gigantic tourist attraction, but many influential bodies from all over the country.

Realising the unrest caused by 'Lot 8', within a week the government had removed the 99 acres of Runnymede from the sale, but having attracted so much attention, its future as an open space was now seen to be under threat. Mrs Normanton, together with the Marquess of Lincolnshire and the Revd. Tranter, immediately formed the Magna Carta Society, which was to act as a guardian of Runnymede.

Elsie Cannon Collection

MAGNA CARTA COMMEMORATION SERVICE   *1924*

Some means of protecting Runnymede against further development had to be found. The Marquess of Lincolnshire had told Mrs Normanton that the prime minister, Rt. Hon. David Lloyd George, had observed the weekend crowds enjoying themselves on Runnymede and therefore thought it might be a good site for a permanent type of funfair. If that was his idea, and the auctioneer was so instructed, an immense price might be obtained and be of great financial benefit to the tenants on Runnymede. Revd. Tranter made his intentions quite clear at a meeting of the League of Nations, where he humerously threatened to 'throw into the river Thames any auctioneer who should attempt to sell Runnymede'. Following the formation of an Egham committee, the Magna Carta Society decided that an annual meeting to commemorate Magna Carta should be held on Runnymede in order to keep the work of the Society in the public eye. At the first meeting, held on 14 June 1923, the Marquess of Lincolnshire delivered a strong plea for the retention of Runnymede as a permanent national possession. The 1924 meeting, pictured here, attracted world-wide attention, particularly in the American press. A number of eminent speakers were secured subsequently, and for many years, a message from King George V was read to the congregation. In 1935 the BBC Regional Service broadcast a service dedicated to Magna Carta live from Egham church.
The Egham Museum Trust

ALBERT CECIL TRANTER, *(1879-1947)*

A C Tranter became vicar of Egham in 1918. He is seen here, with shields of the Magna Carta barons, in Egham church in 1936. He died in Egham Cottage Hospital on 31 January 1947, aged 67.

TICKET FOR THE 1933 MAGNA CARTA COMMEMORATION SERVICE Richard Williams Collection

URBAN HANLON BROUGHTON

Born in Worcester on 12 April 1857, Urban Hanlon Broughton studied engineering at the University of London under the civil engineers Law and Thomas. On leaving university he worked on a variety of projects including the railway, drainage systems and dock works. In 1887 he moved to America where he became engaged in a variety of activities, including engineering, manufacturing, mining and the American railways. Whilst in America, he met and married the New York heiress, Cara Leland. They had two sons, Urban Huttleston Rogers, born August 1896, and Henry Rogers born January 1900. The family returned to England in 1912 and in 1915 Urban Hanlon was elected Conservative MP for Preston. In 1918 the family moved to Park Close in Englefield Green, Surrey, near to the meadows at Runnymede. Urban Hanlon Broughton died suddenly in January 1929, shortly before he was due to be elevated to the peerage. He was 71 years old.

CARA BROUGHTON

Following the death of her husband, Cara Broughton was created Lady Fairhaven in his honour and their eldest son, Urban Huttleston Rogers Broughton, made the first Lord Fairhaven. The family was determined to create a lasting memorial to Urban Broughton and decided upon the lands at Runnymede because, despite their historical significance, they were still under threat from developers. During 1930 two trustees, Sir Reginald Poole (representing the London solicitors Lewis and Lewis) and A C Tranter, vicar of Egham, began to acquire land at Runnymede, later to be transferred to the National Trust. By 1931 most of the land at Runnymede and Long Mead had been purchased. They failed only to secure two narrow strips at the eastern (Staines) end and a stretch bordering the Thames at the western entrance to Long Mead. After successful negotiations involving some twelve separate transactions, 182½ acres of land were given to the National Trust on 7 August 1931, ensuring the famous meadow protection against development for all time. Lady Cara died in 1939.

Portraits reproduced by kind permission of Lord Fairhaven/The National Trust

THE PAVILIONS AND COTTAGES AT RUNNYMEDE

In 1931 Sir Edwin Lutyens was commissioned by the Fairhavens to design suitable buildings to mark the two entrances to Runnymede. This he did in the form of two pavilions (or kiosks, sometimes referred to locally as 'Pepperpots') for the eastern (Staines) entrance and two cottages (or lodges) for the western approach from Windsor. Each pair of buildings was constructed either side of the A308, Windsor Road, and would not only define the boundaries of Runnymede but also serve to remind visitors of the meadow's history. There was some opposition to the scheme locally, mainly from those who feared more building would follow. Work began on both sites in December 1931 and was completed by the following May. The octagonal pavilions at the Staines entrance to Runnymede were designed so that they could be used for the sale of refreshments. They are built of multi-coloured brick with stone dressings and red tiles. The wooden window frames are finished in cream to contrast with the green shutters and doors. A 4.5 metre high Portland stone pillar was erected close to each pavilion and carries an inscription, part of which reads 'the Meadows of Historic Interest were gladly offered to the National Trust on December 18th 1929 in perpetual memory of Urban Hanlon Broughton'. Each pavilion was originally positioned about 50 metres to the east of their present position, towards Staines, but were relocated in January 1966 to allow for minor road realignment.

The cottages at the western approach are built of the same materials as the pavilions and are finished in the same colours. One of these single story buildings was intended to provide an office and a public convenience. The other was designed to be used as a Keeper's cottage. The cottage nearest the river was once used as a small museum but is now used just for storage. Its neighbour remains the National Trust tearoom, which it has been for some time, although there have been plans recently to move this facility into the other cottage. Like the pavilions, each cottage has an accompanying Portland stone pillar and carries a similar inscription to those at the Staines end. In a formal opening ceremony on 8 July 1932 the Prince of Wales, later Edward VIII, simultaneously unveiled the two pillars at the Windsor entrance. Just hours before the ceremony vandals had sprayed the pillars and the walls of the cottages with creosote. It was impossible to clean the stonework in time for the royal visitor's arrival although attempts were made to hide as much of the damage as possible with evergreen shrubs. After weeks of experimenting with different chemicals the stonework was satisfactorily cleaned during September 1932.
Richard Williams

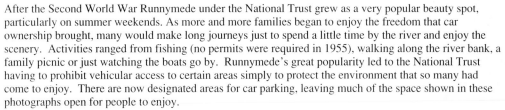

AUGUST BANK HOLIDAY *1955*

After the Second World War Runnymede under the National Trust grew as a very popular beauty spot, particularly on summer weekends. As more and more families began to enjoy the freedom that car ownership brought, many would make long journeys just to spend a little time by the river and enjoy the scenery. Activities ranged from fishing (no permits were required in 1955), walking along the river bank, a family picnic or just watching the boats go by. Runnymede's great popularity led to the National Trust having to prohibit vehicular access to certain areas simply to protect the environment that so many had come to enjoy. There are now designated areas for car parking, leaving much of the space shown in these photographs open for people to enjoy.

The Egham Museum Trust

MAGNA CARTA CELEBRATIONS *1986*

With Runnymede now safely in the hands of the National Trust, the work of the Magna Carta Society had mainly been achieved. A C Tranter, vicar of Egham and staunch supporter, had died in January 1947 and Mrs Helena Normanton resigned as secretary in 1953, aged 70. In 1957 the Magna Carta Society was suceeded by the Magna Carta Trust, who set out with a wider brief to perpetuate the principles of Magna Carta and preserve the sites associated with it. These sites were named as St Edmundsbury, Canterbury, London, St. Albans and Runnymede. It was decided that each location should take it in turns to commemorate Magna Carta every three years and as part of this cycle Runnymede hosted the event in 1986. The celebrations culminated in a commemoration service on Runnymede attended by the mayors from other towns with Magna Carta connections. From left to right are Ted Andrews, Runnymede Borough Council; Maud Austin, Mayor of Runnymede; Lord Donaldson, Master of the Rolls, and Nicholas Burt carrying an umbrella to shield the Magna Carta document (on loan from the British Library) from direct sunlight. Future celebrations are scheduled for London in 1995, St Albans in 1998, Runnymede 2001, St Edmundsbury 2004 and Canterbury 2007.

John Hardaker

PROPOSED VISITORS' CENTRE - *June 1995*

During 1995 an ambitious £3.5 million project was launched by Runnymede Borough Council to create a better interpretation of the Runnymede Meadow and perhaps include an Education and Heritage Centre. One proposal, shown here, is to build a Centre near to the present Pleasure Grounds at Milson's Point, although no scheme will be finally approved until after a period of public consultation. It is hoped that it will be financed by the Millenium Commission as well as with contributions from corporate sponsors, City institutions and interested American groups. Whichever scheme is adopted, Runnymede Borough Council are anxious to work closely with The National Trust, The Magna Carta Trust and the Kennedy Trust in order to achieve the most appropriate tribute to Magna Carta.

Artist's impression - Runnymede Borough Council

The author wishes to point out that this proposal was publicised just days before this book went to press and is included for historical interest only.

AERIAL VIEW OF LONG MEAD looking east c 1949

RUNNYMEDE PAGEANT 1934

By the 1930s, historical pageants were proving very popular in Britain. They had begun in this format at Sherborne, Dorset, as part of the celebrations commemorating the 750th anniversary of the school in 1905. Pageant sites were usually chosen because of their historical background making Runnymede a perfect location. A pageant had been suggested to commemorate the 700th anniversary of Magna Carta but although plans were taking shape it was later abandoned as the First World War continued into 1915. Runnymede had to wait a further 19 years before Lady Enid de Chair, determined to raise money for local charities, rekindled the pageant idea on this historic site. Lady de Chair was the wife of Admiral Sir Dudley de Chair, a former governor of New South Wales, who on their return to England, settled in Virginia Water nearby.
During the autumn of 1933 Lady de Chair approached Gwen Lally, Britain's most successful Pageant Master, with the idea of a pageant at Runnymede. Miss Lally was most enthusiastic and accepted the post of Pageant Master without hesitation. The National Trust, keen to make use of their recently acquired gift, suggested Long Mead as the most favourable site, which it was, but the idea aroused some amusement locally that the Runnymede Pageant should be held on Long Mead! Much work had to be done. There was little more than eight months in which to put together one of the most spectacular pageants of the era. By early 1934 £6000 had been raised from local sources as a guarantee fund. Many of the costumes were being made at organised sewing circles, one press report saying that over 40,000 garments were needed. The Pageant Week, 9 - 16 June was chosen to coincide with the Royal Ascot Race Meeting, thus taking advantage of the additional visitors to the area. It did however, prevent the royal patrons, the Prince of Wales and the Duke and Duchess of York, from attending any of the performances. By the end of January, eight episodes had been allocated to local districts, involving a total of 5,000 performers.

LADY ENID DE CHAIR, PAGEANT CHAIRMAN

The Egham Museum Trust

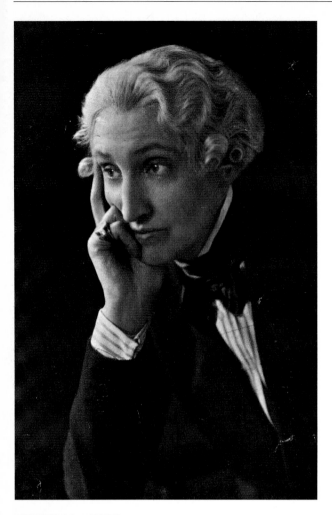

GWEN LALLY, *Pageant Master*

The success of the Runnymede Pageant was virtually assured with in appointment of Gwen Lally as Pageant Master. Her record of nine highly successful productions throughout England during the previous ten years, made her the natural choice. She was born in March 1882, the daughter of Jocelyn Henry Speck, Canon of St Albans, and grew up in the theatre, acting in Shakespearian plays at Her Majesty's Theatre and the Old Vic. She was christened Gwendoline Rosalie Lally Tollandal and used Lally, her grandmother's name, as her stage name. She always dressed in masculine clothes and once claimed that throughout her career she never wore a skirt on stage. She produced her last pageant in Poole, Dorset, in 1952 and was awarded the OBE in 1954. She died in April 1963 aged 81.
Richard Williams Collection

PAGEANT POSTER

A competition was set to design a poster for the forthcoming pageant. It attracted a large number of entries which were judged locally by Gwen Lally, Sir Dudley and Lady Enid de Chair on 9 February 1934. The winning entry was submitted by a Mr Gayes, his design also being used on the cover on the pageant souvenir programme. In order to reach as many people as possible posters were displayed on ocean-going liners and one brewery company even offered to advertise the pageant on their delivery vans.
The Egham Museum Trust

PAGEANT

Patrons:
H.R.H. THE PRINCE OF WALES
T.R.H. THE DUKE & DUCHESS OF YORK

HON. ORGANISER:
LADY DE CHAIR

PAGEANT MASTER:
GWEN LALLY

JUNE 9 TO 16
OF
RUNNYMEDE

PRESS COVERAGE

The combination of Runnymede as a venue and Gwen Lally as Pageant Master ensured that the event would receive plenty of media attention. The Prince of Wales had the idea that a film should be made of the Pageant so that the people of the Dominions and Colonies could enjoy the spectacle. The public houses in Old Windsor were granted all day opening during Pageant Week and there were even rumours that the Pageant Master had hired the Loch Ness Monster for a guest appearance!

Colour photography was in its infancy and natural colour photographs, as they were called, were just beginning to appear in select national magazines. With all its colourful costumes, the Runnymede Pageant became a target for centrefold coverage and these two groups, photographed during rehearsals, provide a rare and early example of colour reproduction. In one, the Plantagenet episode, a tournament in the time of Edward III is performed by the Windsor and District group. The other shows a Tudor scene with Henry VIII and members of the Virginia Water group.

Richard Williams Collection

A TICKET TO THE RUNNYMEDE PAGEANT

The Egham Museum Trust

ADMISSION TICKET with RAIL COUPON

This part to be retained by Spectator

PAGEANT OF RUNNYMEDE

(In aid of Charities and Hospitals of the District)

On the Historic Meadow of Runnymede,
Egham, Surrey,

Saturday, June 9th to Saturday, June 16th
INCLUSIVE

Gates open 6-30 p.m.   Commence 7-30 p.m.

Thursday, June 14, 1934
Available this date only

Evening   STAND   BLOCK

Row and
Seat No.   **L 5**   **A**   **3**

Price 5/- Including Tax

NO MONEY RETURNED

DORLING & CO. (EPSOM), LTD.

RUNNYMEDE PAGEANT

June 9th to 16th, 1934, excluding Sunday, June 10th.

This portion of the Ticket surrendered at the Booking Office or at Railway Stations within a radius of 80 miles of Staines or Egham will obtain a Cheap Day Ticket to Staines or Egham at the Single Fare for the Double Journey : fractions of 1d. to be charged as 1d. Payment to be made at time of Booking. Children under 14 years of age Half-Fare. Special concessions may also be obtained from certain Motor Transport Companies on production of this Voucher.

MAGNA CARTA BARONS

Rehearsals began in earnest during March and the Staines and Egham News, not surprisingly, concentrated on the Magna Carta episode being performed by the Egham and Wraysbury group. This is one of the many photographs published in the weeks leading up to the opening day in June.

The chain mail worn by the barons in this episode was all made from knitted string sprayed with aluminium paint. Pageant Week itself was hot and sunny and many performers were feeling uncomfortable by the end of the day, particularly those who had walked to and from the arena in full costume.

There were two performances daily, at 2.30 pm and 7.30 pm (except, of course, Sunday 10 June). The afternoon sessions were mainly attended by children from local schools who paid 6d (2½p) each for admission. Work prevented a large number of men from taking part in the afternoon performances, their places often being taken by their wives or mothers.

The Egham Museum Trust

ELEPHANTS ON RUNNYMEDE?

Apart from estimating that about 5,000 performers would take part in the Pageant, the press also reported that something like 200 horses would be needed and appealed to any horse owners living nearby to contact Major N Bray MC, who had accepted the post of Master of the Horse. On 28 February all three national evening papers featured an article about the Revd. J R James of Staines who had been seen riding an elephant during rehearsals for the Staines episode. It transpired that four elephants from Bertram Mills Circus were to be loaned to the Pageant, but the authorities later thought better of it and considered the problems of keeping these large animals for a week on Runnymede as being prohibitive.

The Egham Museum Trust

THE OPENING CEREMONY

After months of hard work and numerous rehearsals, the Runnymede Pageant was officially opened at 2.30pm on Saturday 9 June by the Lord Mayor of London, Sir Charles Collett. The day began with a civic luncheon in the Guildhall, Windsor, given by the Mayor of Windsor, Councillor G E Short. Among the invited guests were dignitaries from towns and cities with historic connections with Runnymede and included the Mayors of Leicester, Reading, Bury St. Edmunds, St. Albans and the Deputy Mayor of Canterbury. Following lunch, the company were driven in procession by car to Runnymede where they were met by Admiral Sir Dudley de Chair, the Honorary Marshall. It was originally intended that the journey should be made down the river Thames by motor launch but this was later deemed to be too time consuming. After a short speech by the chairman of Egham Urban District Council, Mr F H White, Sir Charles Collett declared the Runnymede Pageant open, noting in his address that ' In this pageant you have not a kingdom for a stage but an empire'. The mayoral party, dressed in robes, occupied the Royal Box for the opening performance.
The Egham Museum Trust

THE PROLOGUE

The Prologue and the Epilogue were both especially written for the Runnymede Pageant by the poet John Drinkwater and formed the only narrative in the entire production. The eight main episodes were all performed in mime to the music of the Band of the Life Guards under the direction of Lt. S S Smith. The Prologue was spoken by the Spirit of the Thames, a part taken on separate occasions by Dame Sybil Thorndike DBE, Lady Forbes Robertson and Mrs Lyster Blandy. For this purpose a microphone was concealed in the chariot carrying the Spirit of the Thames and linked to the arena Tannoy system. This ensured that the Prologue could be heard by the entire audience which was considered to be quite an innovation at that time.
The Egham Museum Trust

EPISODE 1 - THE ROMAN CONQUEST OF BRITAIN *AD 44*

The first episode, performed by the Staines and Ashford group, portrayed what life might have been like in a small British homestead near the Thames between Staines and Windsor during the Roman Conquest.
In AD 43, Emperor Claudius had sent an army of 40,000 men under the command of Aulus Plactius to conquer Britain. By AD 44 the Second Legion were marching up the Thames valley under their general, Vespasian. They rarely found much resistance to their superior weapons which included powerful catapults and often a number of elephants. It was for this episode that these large animals had originally been intended (see page 40). The episode culminated with an entire village population taking refuge in their chieftain's fort. Initially the Roman army had met with more resistance than they expected, but following the death of the British chieftain the Roman legionaries continued their march towards Silchester.
The Egham Museum Trust

EPISODE 2 - THE SACKING OF CHERTSEY ABBEY *AD 884*

The Benedictine abbey of Chertsey had been founded in AD 666 by St Erkenwald. According to the abbey's own chronicler, a Danish fleet sailed up the river Thames in 884 and killed the 90 monks at the abbey for refusing to leave their posts. The abbey itself was badly damaged by fire, its possessions burned and crops destroyed. After many years the abbey at Chertsey was refounded in the 10th century during the time of Aethelwold, Bishop of Winchester. According to many visitors to the Pageant, this episode was much enjoyed. On a given signal from the Pageant Master, Gwen Lally, men inside the replica of Chertsey Abbey, built on the edge of the arena, removed the roof panels using long wooden poles. A great deal of smoke was generated within the arena, adding to the general excitement.
The Egham Museum Trust

EPISODE 3 -
THE SEALING OF MAGNA CARTA *1215*

It was appropriate that the Magna Carta episode should be allocated to the Egham and Wraysbury group. They were joined by players from Old Windsor and Thorpe to recreate the meeting between King John and the 25 barons that had taken place on the same meadow 719 years earlier. Some of those taking part claimed to be direct descendents from those who attended the original ceremony in 1215. This was the first episode to have a central figure, King John, who was played on separate occasions by Lord St. John of Bletso and J Carew Jones. Many of the leading roles in later episodes were taken by the titled gentry, much to the annoyance of some of the 'lower orders'. It was conveniently forgotten that but for their generosity the Pageant might not have taken place at all. One of the hardest workers backstage was Mrs Wilkinson, wife of the Egham GP. She was appointed assistant property master for the Pageant because of her great skill as a carpenter. She made King John's chair and dais for the Magna Carta episode and was referred to by an appreciative Gwen Lally as the 'lady with the saw'. Mrs Wilkinson, seen here outside her caravan, also took part in the Magna Carta episode.

The Egham Museum Trust

EPISODE 4 -
A TOURNAMENT AT WINDSOR GIVEN BY KING EDWARD III - *1358*

Tournaments were very popular during the Middle Ages. They not only gave knights the opportunity to prove their skills and advance up the social ladder, but proved also to be a great spectacle. On 23 April 1358, to coincide with St. George's Day, Edward III arranged for a most sumptuous feast and tournament to be held at Windsor. His son, Edward the Black Prince, was in attendance, having been the victor at Poitiers in France two years earlier. Two of his prisoners, King John of France and his son Philip, were present at the tournament, but, in the manner of the day, were treated as distinguished guests rather than prisoners. The tiltyard was erected and six courses ridden between the seven combatants. These were the earls of Suffolk, Warwick, March and Salisbury, Lord Stafford and the kings of France and Scotland. After the event, the Black Prince as adjudicator, proclaimed the King of France the winner, for which the king received a rich jewel and a crown of bay from the Queen of Beauty. Most of the jousting knights were played by men with army training, but the King of France was played by the Revd. E Dawson Walker, perhaps a former army chaplain.
The Egham Museum Trust

EPISODE 5 -
A TUDOR ENTERTAINMENT - *1522*

No pageant would be complete without an episode featuring King Henry VIII, and at Runnymede the Virginia Water group gave their full attention to one of England's most colourful monarchs. In a number of performances the king was played by Brough Ansdell, an actor who had played the part in several previous pageants. Paul Tingey frequently played the part of Cardinal Wolsey, as he did at some performances on Runnymede, and, with Brough Ansdell, belonged to a small group of professional or semi-professional actors taking part in the pageant.The episode centred around an extravagant Tudor entertainment, given by Henry VIII in order to impress his guest of honour, Charles V, Holy Roman Emperor and King of Spain. It began with the Masque of the Proud Horse, where allegorical figures tamed a high-spirited charger representing France, performed by a horse called Bimbo from the Wentworth Riding School. A musical interlude led by a lady of the Court followed. The final scene began with a dance known as the Two Twelves. The preformers were twelve courtiers dressed in cloth of gold and silver, representing wealth, and twelve ladies wearing gold bonnets, hoods and buskins, representing luxury. The episode concluded with the arrival of a beggar maid for whom the lavishly dressed courtiers deserted their ladies. However their advances were rejected by the beggar maid and King Henry, impressed by this show of loyalty towards him ordered her to be wreathed in garlands from his table.
The Egham Museum Trust

THE HOUSE ON FEET - TUDOR EPISODE

A number of clever ideas were used to change the arena scenery as quickly as possible between episodes, thus ensuring the entire performance ran smoothly. A small arena party, under the direction of the appropriate property master, would be responsible for major items and set them up in the arena as the cast took their places. Smaller items were carried in, almost un-noticed, by the players themselves. But perhaps the most ingenious, and certainly the most amusing, was the 'house on feet'. This model of a Tudor cottage was simply moved by the eight men inside it, by lifting it up and walking to and from its position in the arena.
The Egham Museum Trust

EPISODE 6 - KING CHARLES II HUNTING IN THE ROYAL FOREST - *1670*

At this period, shortly after the Restoration, the boundaries of the Royal Forests extended beyond Bagshot. Swinley Forest was an integral part of Windsor Forest, and the nearby villages were mere hamlets within the forest.

The sixth episode was performed by the Camberley group and began with King Charles II, accompanied by Louise de Kerouaille, being greeted by Sunninghill villagers prior to a hunt in Windsor Forest. The arrival of Nell Gwyn by coach created some tension, before the king made peace between the two rivals. Upon the signal for the hunt to begin, given by the king's Master of the Horse, the king and his courtiers mounted their horses and the cavalcade streamed across the arena and departed. The area was notorious for cut-throats and highwaymen and just as the remaining ladies and gentlemen of the court began to return to their coaches a group of highwaymen appeared. They overpowered the servants with their pistols and began to demand money and valuables from the frightened passengers. The well-known highwayman, Claude Duval, was featured in this episode. He was a Frenchman of humble origin who came to England at the time of the Restoration. Duval was reputed to have frequently invited pretty female travellers to join him in a dance in exchange for the safe return of their belongings. It is thought that he lived near Green Lanes Farm in Windlesham before being caught and hanged in 1670.

The episode concluded happily when the king's hunting party returned from their successful day in the forest carrying a buck slung between two poles. Their celebrations lasted well into the evening.
The Egham Museum Trust

EPISODE 7 -
QUEEN ANNE OPENS ASCOT RACES - *1711*

The announcement of the first horse race to be held at Ascot, appeared in the *London Gazette* on 12 July 1711, which read 'Her Majesty's Plate for 100 guineas will be run for round the new heat (course) on Ascot Common, near Windsor, Tuesday August 7th next by any horse, mare or gelding no more than six years old the grass (year) before as must be certified by the hand of the breeder, carrying 12st to be entered the last day of July at Mr Hancock's at Fern Hill near the starting post.'

In the event, the race was postponed until 11 August, when Queen Anne attended and officially opened the meeting. Seven horses competed for the prize, but despite the winner being introduced to the Queen, we are not told who he was! The photograph shows members of the Ascot group entering the arena with Queen Anne riding in a sedan chair. Some of the stands can be seen in the background. The small 'crow's nest' above the stand, just visible in the top left hand corner, is where Gwen Lally spent the entire performance often shouting her instructions to the performers through a megaphone.

The Egham Museum Trust

EPISODE 8 -
RURAL ENGLAND AFTER WATERLOO - *1817*

The final episode of the Runnymede Pageant was a scene from rural England in 1817 shortly after the Battle of Waterloo and took the form of a village fair. Locally, such fairs were popular in the 17th and 18th centuries, the Black Cherry Fair at Chertsey, the Gypsy Horse Fair at Blackwater and the Staines Fair, all date from this period. Popular attractions included a Punch and Judy show, a number of strolling players with their fit-up theatre, tumblers and pedlars. Pick-pockets mingled with the rich and the poor who were eager to enjoy their day at the fair. During the episode, performed by the Slough and District group, the Duke of Wellington, played alternately by Major Mainwaring Burton and the Revd Mervyn Clare, made a suprise visit on his way to the State Opening of Waterloo Bridge. Afterwards the Duke continued his journey in easy stages to Stratfield Saye Place, a property the government proposed to give him in appreciation of his service to the nation.

Richard Williams Collection

THE GRAND FINALE

Each performance of the Pageant concluded with an Epilogue, written especially for the occasion by John Drinkwater. It was read by either Miss Irene or Miss Violet Vanburgh with the entire company assembled in the arena. It provided a spectacular end to a magnificent show, each performance lasting, on average, three hours. Despite the huge success of the Runnymede Pageant, there was a sad outcome. In February 1935 the Treasury informed the organisers that the full amount of Entertainment Tax would have to be paid because the expenses exceeded 20% of the gross takings. The costs involved in the hiring of horses and costumes, together with the erection of stands etc. far exceeded the estimated costs and instead of making a sizeable profit for local charities, the Pageant lost about £300. The pageant committee were considering an appeal but no further mention was made in the local press.

The Egham Museum Trust

AERIAL VIEW OF THE PAGEANT ARENA

The Pageant arena was situated towards the Egham end of Long Mead and occupied approximately five acres of land, just below the slopes of Cooper's Hill.

This aerial view shows the covered stands backing onto the Windsor Road (A308). The large preparation area is behind the open stands on the right and the Pageant Fort gateway, through which the performers entered the arena, is in the foreground. A suprising number of cars for 1934 can be seen in the car park away to the left. It was estimated that nearly 90,000 spectators attended the fourteen performances, with many evening shows being completely sold out.

The stands used for the Pageant were hired from H W Diamond, a company based in Leicester. Planning permission for their temporary erection was granted on 3 April and their removal completed by 7 July 1934. The difficulty of providing stabling for some 200 horses throughout a hot and humid week was not without its problems. However, the public were no doubt reassured by the footnote in the Pageant programme that said 'In the interests of public health, this Pageant is being disinfected throughout with Jeyes Fluid'.

The Egham Museum Trust

Reproduced by kind permission of the Imperial War Museum

BOEING FLYING FORTRESS A/C 42-31178 B 17 G

Like many small towns in the south of England, Egham suffered its share of damage in the Second World War. Few towns, however, can claim the excitement that was generated locally when a Boeing Flying Fortress crash landed on Long Mead during the early evening of 31 December 1943. The aircraft had taken off from Bassingbourn in Cambridgeshire, as one of a number despatched to French targets by the US 8th Air Force, to bomb the airfields of Merignac at Bordeaux and Chateaubernard at Cognac occupied by the Luftwaffe. Weather conditions that day were poor. The cloud base was between 500 and 800 feet, winds were 50mph and visibility varied from 500 to 2,500 yards. On its return to England, the Flying Fortress left its formation and descended through cloud, flying at altitudes between 300 and 500 feet, with the pilot looking for a suitable landing site. Dusk was approaching and the crew, who were without navigation or communications radio, clearly had no idea where they were. The time was about 5.30pm and, because British Summer Time was kept throughout the year, there was just sufficient light for the aircraft to be seen. It roughly followed the river Thames from Staines before finally coming to rest on Long Mead, opposite Magna Carta Island. Afterwards it was discovered that the aircraft had 300 gallons of fuel on board, which luckily did not catch fire, and all ten members of the crew escaped unhurt. Initially the crew thought they had landed in France but were overjoyed to find they were in England. They celebrated the New Year at the nearby Bells of Ouseley public house. By the time the head of the local Civil Defence arrived to guard the aircraft, a number of Egham residents had plundered the wreckage for souvenirs. Much of the material taken was later returned to Egham Police Station, following an appeal made by a member of the War Reserve Police Force. The aircraft, probably dismantled between 1-3rd January 1944, was removed in sections on two Queen Mary trailers.

CREW OF A/C 42-29487 DFK RITZY BLITZ B 17 F

Eight of the crew who crash landed on Long Mead were assigned to another aircraft, A/C 42-29487 DFK Ritzy Blitz. Just a few days later, on 11 January 1944, this aircraft crashed, killing five of the crew, the remaining five being taken prisoner

BACK ROW, left to right: Sgt James Lascu junior (Radio Operator), Sgt Stanley E Lyttle (not aboard the aircraft which crashed on Long Mead), Sgt Walter P Williams (Armament Engineer), Sgt William O Francisco (Gunner) and George M Richardson (Armament Radio Operator).

FRONT ROW, left to right: 2nd Lt Carey S Goodwin junior (Navigator), 2nd Lt Donald W Jones (Co-pilot), 2nd Lt Wayne D Hedglin (Pilot), John E McKewen (not aboard the aircraft which crashed on Long Mead) and Sgt Cody L Wolf (Engineer).

The two crew members who were aboard the aircraft which crashed on Long Mead but not pictured here were Technical Sgt Robert W White (Navigator Gunner) and Staff Sgt Donald L Hahlen (Gunner).
The Egham Museum Trust

RUNNYMEDE HOUSE   *1984*

Runnymede House is situated in four acres of grounds overlooking Runnymede at the western approach. The plot and the adjacent fifteen acres of pasture form part of a site known in the 13th century as Lodderlake-hatch, a point at which the three counties of Berkshire, Buckinghamshire and Surrey met. The lake itself was close to the foot of Priest Hill and was formed by the damming up of the Tilebedburn, a stream dividing Berkshire and Surrey. Runnymede House was given its name by the Nevile Reid family during the 19th century, although this and an earlier property had been called Lodderlake during the ownership of the Leigh family of Ankerwyke.
Richard Williams

MAGNA CARTA MEMORIAL STONE

The 19th century Surrey historian, E W Brayley, wrote in his book that although it had been 'several times in contemplation to erect a column at Runnymede as a perpetual memorial of the Great Event....either from insufficient means or a reproachful deficiency of patriotism, no effectual steps have hitherto been taken to accomplish that desirable object'. Like us today, the Victorians did not know the precise spot where King John met with the 25 barons and probably chose not to guess for fear of being proved wrong later. In 1911 Capt Symons-Jeune and his family moved into Runnymede House and shortly after the First World War commissioned a single stone to be erected at the eastern extremity of his land as a memorial to Magna Carta. It is quite likely that this was a positive reaction to the threatened sale of Runnymede in 1921.

The stone faced directly onto Long Mead and was inscribed 'Very near to this spot was sealed MAGNA CARTA confirming rights which were in peril and won from King John by the BISHOPS and BARONS for the abiding benefit of the PEOPLE OF ENGLAND and later of the British Dominions and United States of America'.

The stone can still be seen, although the inscription is now partly illegible, just beyond the National Trust tearoom car park at the western end of Long Mead.
Richard Williams

THE COMMONWEALTH AIR FORCES MEMORIAL

Built on a spur of Cooper's Hill overlooking Runnymede, the Commonwealth Air Forces Memorial commemorates the lives of 20,455 personnel who perished whilst serving with, or in association with, the Royal Air Force and have no known graves. The memorial was built by the Imperial War Graves Commission, following recommendations made by the Air Council in February 1948, and is dedicated to the airmen and women who lost their lives while serving from bases in the United Kingdom and north-west Europe.

The six acre site, with its commanding views towards Windsor to the west and Heathrow to the east, was generously donated to the Commission by Sir Eugen and Lady Effie Millington-Drake. Work began on the site in 1950 with the main contract going to Holloway Brothers of London. The blocks of Portland stone used in the construction were prepared in a numbered sequence before delivery to the site for assembly. The memorial was opened by Her Majesty, Queen Elizabeth II on 17 October 1953 and afterwards consecrated by the Archbishop of Canterbury in the presence of about 25,000 people seated in a great semi-circle. The memorial was awarded the Bronze Medal of the Royal Institute of British Architects (RIBA) for the best building erected in the south of England during the eight years ending in December 1955.
Richard Williams

ENTRANCE TO THE MEMORIAL

Entrance to the grounds of the memorial is through two solid English oak gates which lead the visitor into the beautifully maintained gardens, with cut lawns and tidy flower beds. Either side of the pathway leading to the memorial is a line of chestnut trees, planted in the autumn of 1990 to replace the original avenue of silver birch trees. During the re-landscaping, two large banks of rhododendrons were also removed and replaced with a number of flower beds on either side of the pathway.

The memorial entrance is through a central arch of three, each containing glazed double doors bearing some fine nickel-bronze work. This is repeated in the panes above each doorway. Above the triple arched portico is a great stone eagle, the work of Edmond Burton, below which is inscribed the Royal Air Force motto 'Per Ardua Ad Astra'. A register containing the names of all those commemorated at Runnymede is permanently available for reference just inside the entrance.
Richard Williams

EDWARD MAUFE RA

The architect for the Commonwealth Air Force Memorial was Edward Maufe, a Yorkshireman much honoured by his profession. Born at Ilkley on 12 December 1883, he was educated locally at Wharfedale School until 1899 when he was sent to serve a five year pupilage with the London achitect, William A Pite. He became an associate member of the RIBA in 1910 and immediately set up in practice on his own. Following a number of prestigious commissions, Maufe won the competition for Guildford Cathedral in 1932, his design being preferred to nearly 200 other entries. The Second World War meant that its completion was delayed until 1961. Between 1943 and 1969, Maufe was first principal architect UK and then Chief Architect and artistic advisor to the Imperial (later Commonwealth) War Graves Commission. He was elected Associate of the Royal Academy (ARA) in 1938, RA in 1947 and knighted in 1954 for his services to the War Graves Commission. Sir Edward Maufe died on 12 December 1974, his 91st birthday, at his restored farmhouse at Shepherd's Hill, Buxted, Sussex.
Photograph reproduced by kind permission of the British Architectural Library/RIBA

THE CLOISTERS

Surrounding the quadrangle on all four sides are the cloisters, containing stone panels inscribed with all the names of those remembered at Runnymede. The panels are arranged on either side of long narrow windows so as to allow in sufficient light for the incised names to be read.

The lives commemorated are made up as follows:-

Royal Air Force	15,308
Royal Canadian Air Force	3,072
Royal Australian Air Force	1,403
Royal New Zealand Air Force	583
Royal Air Force of Newfoundland	26
South African Air Force	16
Women's Auxillary Air Force	10
Air Transport Auxillary	10
Ferry Command	9
Royal Indian Air Force	7
British Overseas Airways Corporation	7
Air Training Corps	4
Total	**20,455**

The arms of Great Britain, Canada, Australia, New Zealand, South Africa, India and Pakistan form colourful ceiling panels beneath the cloisters. Small five-pointed stars are carved into the capitals of each supporting column and escallops, a sign of immortality, are shown on the front edge of the stone seats.

Richard Williams

THE QUADRANGLE AND TOWER

The double front doors of the memorial lead into the quadrangle. The central feature is the Stone of Remembrance, a single block of Portland stone bearing the inscription 'Their name liveth for evermore' It is reached on either side by a solid stone pathway surrounded by neatly kept segments of lawn.

On the northern side of the quadrangle is the tower. Above the central doorway are three stone figures by the sculptor Vernon Hill representing Justice, Victory and Courage. Near the top of the tower are five picture windows which allow light into an upper story reached by an internal stone staircase. The cloisters continue round into two curved wings, either side of the tower, each terminating in a small balcony with views across Runnymede. To the right of the tower can be seen the roofs of the cloisters, finished in Westmorland green slate. At the top of the tower is the Royal Air Force crown of blue and gold stars and wings, held high above the memorial on a slender pedestal. The large central star is often illuminated after dark.

Richard Williams

THE TOWER INTERIOR

Within the tower is a small area with oak chairs and kneelers, for rest and contemplation. The ceiling above is painted with four angels and clusters of heavenly bodies upon a pale blue background. A stone spiral staircase leads to a small viewing area where the Great North Window, engraved by John Hutton, can be seen. It has as its inscription part of the 139th Psalm, beginning 'If I climb up into heaven, Thou art there'. Two angels with trumpets support the scroll, above them are the sun and moon with the wings of the morning in the centre. Engraved designs of vapour trails, copied from those made by aircraft in the skies over England during the Battle of Britain, are shown in single panes above the angels.
Richard Williams

THE GREAT NORTH WINDOW   *Pitkin Pictorials Ltd*

VIEW FROM THE TOP OF THE MEMORIAL

The climb to the top of the memorial tower is rewarded with a breath-taking view across Runnymede,
seen here on a clear June day in 1988.
Richard Williams

THE AMERICAN BAR ASSOCIATION MEMORIAL

Following the invitation to hold their 80th Annual Meeting in London during 1957, the American Bar Association sought authority to build a permanent memorial to Magna Carta at Runnymede. For this purpose, the Egham Urban District Council gave the Association a one acre piece of gently sloping grassland, adjacent to the National Trust land at Runnymede, overlooked by mature oak trees. It was to be a worthy and lasting tribute by American lawyers to an event which was considered by both Britain and America to be the origin of 'Freedom under Law'. The memorial is maintained by The Magna Carta Trust under the Chairmanship of the Master of the Rolls.

Richard Williams

THE MEMORIAL AND DEDICATION CEREMONY

The memorial was designed by Sir Edward Maufe RA, architect of the Commonwealth Air Force Memorial nearby. The centre of the memorial is a great pillar of Cornish granite, which is inscribed 'To Commemorate Magna Carta, Symbol of Freedom Under Law'. This is mounted centrally on a stone base under a star-spangled blue dome, with an eye of light at the centre. The dome is supported by eight hexagonal stone columns which join an internal frieze around the dome, the latter carrying the inscription 'Erected by the American Bar Association, A tribute to Magna Carta, Symbol of Freedom Under Law'. A ceremony of dedication was held on Runnymede at 4pm on Sunday, 28 July 1957 in the presence of over 5000 people. The dedication was conducted by the Revd Canon J de Firth, Master of the Temple, with the Hon David F Maxwell, President of the ABA presiding. Addresses were delivered by the Hon E Smythe Gambrell, Immediate Past President of the ABA; the Hon Lord Evershed, Master of the Rolls; the Hon Charles S F Rhyne, Chairman of the House of Delegates of the ABA and Chairman of the Magna Carta Commemoration Committee and the Rt Hon Sir Hartley Shawcross QC, MP, Chairman of the General Council of the Bar of England and Wales. A programme of music was played by the 751 Air Force Band, 3rd USAF.

Richard Williams
The Egham Museum Trust

THE KENNEDY MEMORIAL

ohn F Kennedy, 35th President of the United States of merica, was assassinated on 22 November 1963 while on a isit to Dallas in Texas. Shortly afterwards the British overnment decided to bequeath 'an acre of land' (actually ree acres) overlooking Runnymede to the American people r all time as a memorial to their former President. It was esigned by landscape architect Geoffrey A Jellicoe, and has its central feature a seven ton block of Portland stone representing a catafalque borne on the shoulders of the multitude. The stone was taken from the same Whitbed quarry that had produced material for St Paul's Cathedral some 300 years earlier. The incised text is the work of sculptor Alan Collins and includes a passage from President Kennedy's inaugural address in January 1961. The photograph shows the work being carried out in a shed especially erected on the site.

Richard Williams
Associated Press

THE KENNEDY MEMORIAL

The design chosen by Geoffrey Jellicoe for the Kennedy Memorial is based on a parallel landscape of John Bunyan's *Pilgrim's Progress* and is one of life, death and spirit. The entrance is through a wicket gate on the edge of Runnymede, opposite Magna Carta Island. A pathway of more than 60,000 individually axe-hewn granite setts, representing a multitude of pilgrims, winds gently upwards through the 'wildwood of life'. The surface is intentionally rough and as the slope increases, a number of shallow steps, one for each year of the President's life, is incorporated into the pathway. On reaching the top, the granite setts widen out to form an area beneath the stone, to receive standing visitors, with five Portland stone steps providing access to the stone itself. The analogy is concluded by a pathway towards the future and President Kennedy's concept of Law and Order.
Richard Williams

GEOFFREY JELLICOE

Geoffrey Jellicoe, CBE, FRIBA, had designed gardens for Sandringham, The Royal Lodge at Windsor and the central area of the Royal Horticultural Society gardens at Wisley. Locally, he designed housing at the Chertsey Civic Centre. His *Studies in Landscape Design* published 1959-70 in three volumes, is widely acclaimed as a standard work. He was knighted in 1979.
Photograph reproduced by permission of the British Architectural Library/RIBA

THE KENNEDY MEMORIAL

At the end of the pathway two stone seats are embedded in the hillside, symbolising two thrones. The upper seat, with a background of pine trees on the skyline, is the public image of the President, while the secondary seat belongs to his consort. A ha-ha forms the boundary between the memorial and National Trust land at Runnymede in order to minimise the division of land between Great Britain and the United States of America. The cost of the memorial was borne by public subscription following an appeal by the Lord Mayor of London. It is administered by the John F Kennedy Memorial Trust, nine of whose members are British and three American. The memorial stone was unveiled by Her Majesty Queen Elizabeth II on 14 May 1965 in the presence of Mrs Jacqueline Kennedy, her two children John junior and Caroline Kennedy and the late President's two brothers, Robert and Edward. In her speech the Queen said 'Government under the rule of law is a part of the heritage which the people of the United States of America share with us. Therefore it is altogether fitting that this should be the site of Britain's memorial to the late President John F Kennedy.'

The Queen formally handed over the land to Mr Dean Rusk, the United States Secretary of State, representing President Johnson. The ceremony was broadcast on BBC television. In October 1968 the memorial stone was badly damaged by a terrorist bomb, but was later restored leaving little evidence of the blast. Later, in July 1974, vandals pulled the stone to the ground using a steel hawser and daubed it with red paint. Although chipped in the fall, the stone was only superficially damaged and was soon replaced upon its stone cushion.

Richard Williams
P A News

THE NATIONAL TRUST

THIS OAK TREE, PLANTED WITH SOIL FROM JAMESTOWN, VIRGINIA, THE FIRST PERMANENT ENGLISH SETTLEMENT IN THE NEW WORLD, COMMEMORATES THE BICENTENARY OF THE CONSTITUTION OF THE UNITED STATES OF AMERICA. IT STANDS IN ACKNOWLEDGEMENT THAT THE IDEALS OF LIBERTY AND JUSTICE EMBODIED IN THE CONSTITUTION TRACE THEIR LINEAGE THROUGH INSTITUTIONS OF ENGLISH LAW TO THE MAGNA CARTA, SEALED AT RUNNYMEDE ON JUNE 15TH, 1215. PLANTED DECEMBER 2, 1987, BY JOHN O. MARSH, JR., SECRETARY OF THE ARMY OF THE UNITED STATES OF AMERICA.

COMMEMORATIVE OAK TREES

To commemorate the Bicentenary of the Constitution of the United States of America, John O'Marsh, Senior Secretary of the United States Army, planted an oak tree on the edge of Runnymede, close to the American Bar Association Memorial, on 2 December 1987.
Just a few days later, Her Majesty Queen Elizabeth II planted another oak tree close by, this time to mark National Tree Week. The sudden spate of tree planting on Runnymede led people to think that it had something to do with the Great Storm just seven weeks earlier, but both events had been planned several months in advance. The Queen was accompanied by the Duke of Edinburgh and the Premier Baron of England, the Rt Hon the Lord Mowbray and many other barons whose names are associated with Magna Carta. The event had been arranged by the Tree Council, whose chairman, Major General T A Richardson, hoped that by the millenium of Magna Carta in 2215, the tree would have matured to form a backcloth for the anticipated celebrations.
Richard Williams/Vince Smith MBE

INDIAN PRIME MINISTER'S VISIT TO RUNNYMEDE

A third commemorative tree was planted at Runnymede by the Indian Prime Minister, Mr P V Narasihma Rao, on 16 March 1994, during his four day visit to Britain. It was the first time that a visiting head of government had been invited to visit Runnymede. In a brief ceremony, Mr Narasihma Rao planted an English oak within the boundaries of the American Bar Association Memorial, as a mark of India's tribute to the principles of Magna Carta. To the right of the Prime Minister is Air Commodore V K Verma, with Mr R Wangdi of the Indian High Commission on the far right. To complete the ceremony Mr Narasihma Rao unveiled the commemorative plaque shown on the left.
Reproduced by kind permission of India Weekly

EGHAM AND THORPE ROYAL SHOW

By far the biggest event regularly held on Runnymede is the Egham and Thorpe Royal Agricultural and Horticultural Association Show, which takes place annually over the August Bank Holiday weekend. The show began in 1857 as the Egham Agricultural Society, with a ploughing match held on land belonging to Foster Court Farm, off Manorcrofts Road. Part of this land is now occupied by Egham Bowls Club. The show first moved to Runnymede in 1955 when the site was at the Windsor end, but moved the following year to the now familiar Staines end. The venue has been unchanged except for a short period in the 1970s when three other locations were used. The showground, which straddles land held by both the Runnymede Borough Council and the National Trust, is used for a wide variety of events. A large marquee contains a wide range of local produce, all competing for various awards. There are trade stands, snack bars and, in recent years, a local radio station. Association members have their own area next to the main show ring. The many attractions to be seen there include a cattle parade during the first day and vintage cars and motor cycles on the second. Traction engines remain very popular and a number of them can always be found at the eastern end of the showground. Runnymede Borough Council generously provide an area in the large marquee for local groups and charities to use for fund raising and publicity. Vince Smith (left) and Roy Gryngell, seen here, represent the Egham and Staines Conservation Volunteers. Mr Smith was made MBE in the 1995 Queen's Birthday Honours for his tireless conservation work and his assistance with other voluntary organisations. The show provides plenty of entertainment for children ranging from train rides and a bouncy castle to a large fun-fair.

Richard Williams